NEED TO KNOW

BIGFOOT & FRIENDS

Introducing 13 Cryptids You Need to Know

WRITTEN BY
MOLLIE THOMAS

Illustrated by
Wendy Stephens

RP MINIS
PHILADELPHIA

RP Minis®
Hachette Book Group
1290 Avenue of the Americas, New York, NY 10104
www.runningpress.com
@Running_Press

First Edition: September 2025

Published by RP Minis, an imprint of Hachette Book Group, Inc. The RP Minis name and logo is a registered trademark of Hachette Book Group, Inc.

Contact specialmarkets@hbgusa.com regarding special discounts for bulk purchases.

The publisher is not responsible for websites (or their content) that are not owned by the publisher.

Design by Jenna McBride

ISBN: 979-8-89414-068-1

Made in Dongguan, China (HKD) 11/25 #02

Contents

What Is a Cryptid, Anyway?

This whole tiny book is a complete celebration of cryptids. What is a cryptid, you ask? A cryptid is an animal (or thing) said to be real but whose existence has never been absolutely, resolutely, indisputably proven.

Cryptozoologists (gesundheit!) study cryptids. In many cases, they have dedicated their lives to finding these characters and proving their existence.

By their very being (or not), cryptids inspire a desire to believe in something, optimism in the face of denial, and the reminder to never give up. We can all learn a little something from these cryptids.

Let's go on a journey, a path of possibility, and say hello to your new favorite cryptids.

INTRODUCING THE CAST OF CRYPTID CHARACTERS

CRYPTID 1:
Bigfoot

Of all the cryptids possibly gallivanting around this great earth, Bigfoot might be the most popular. Also known as Sasquatch, this eight-foot-tall hairy, ape-human is said to roam the woods scaring hikers, campers, and loggers aplenty. Although most often seen in the Pacific Northwest region of the United States, sightings have been reported all over the US and Canada—and even across the globe. That's one well-traveled 'tid. Recorded findings of Bigfoot date back to the 1800s and likely even earlier based on verbal lore.

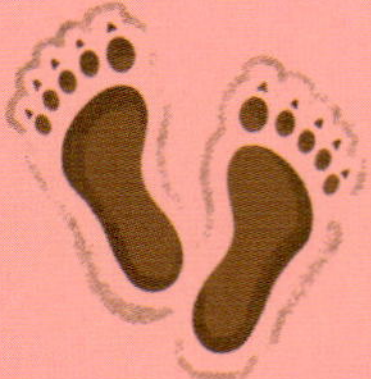

CRYPTID 2:
Mothman

The second character in our Cryptid Cast is similarly solitary and scary but much less widespread. Mothman was first seen by two couples in the year 1966 in West Virginia. The foursome reported to the local paper they saw a large man-bird-like creature with wings and glowing red eyes. According to the group, it chased them, made a loud screeching sound, and flew "100 miles an hour."

CRYPTID 3:
The Jersey Devil

The Jersey Devil, also known as the Leeds Devil, dates back to the year 1735 when Jane Leeds ("Mother Leeds") became pregnant with a thirteenth child. Frustrated at being pregnant yet again, she cursed the unborn child, calling it the "devil." According to folklore, she went into labor on a stormy night and gave birth to a baby, which transformed into an evil creature. Some say it has hooves, wings, and a goat's head, or maybe it's a horse head. It has four feet, or maybe just two. Definitely a tail. Maybe it's forked. Or maybe not. The origin story and details of the Jersey Devil are extremely varied, but one thing is known for sure (though, to be clear, not proven at all) the creature lives in the Pines of South

Jersey and haunts residents and visitors alike.

CRYPTID 4:

The Loch Ness Monster

Say hello to our first Euro-Cryptid: the Loch Ness Monster, also lovingly known as "Nessie." This long-necked beast reportedly dates back to the seventh century AD when a man was attacked by a creature in the River Ness in Scotland. But the lake-loving, dino-like sea creature gained

popularity in the 1930s when multiple sightings were reported and the first photo was published, taken by Hugh Gray in 1933.

CRYPTID 5: Yeti

Not to be confused with the outdoor brand everyone loves to show off, the Yeti is a large, hairy beast who looks a lot like Bigfoot but reportedly lives across the ocean in the Himalayan Mountains. He is also sometimes called the Abominable Snowman. Most photos show not the Yeti himself but instead his footprint. Though there have been reports of Yetis eating human flesh, for the most part they're painted in a harmless,

if not positive, light. Some people even worship Yetis, praising them for warding off evil spirits. And who could be scared of the Yeti portrayed in the adorable film *Monsters, Inc.*? So far on our list, the Yeti seems the friendliest.

CRYPTID 6:
El Chupacabra

Y'all, we've got a baby cryptid here. El Chupacabra was first introduced to the Cryptid Cast of Characters in 1995! So new! Spanish for "goat-sucker" (*chupa*: "sucks"; *cabra*: "goat"), Chupacabras are said to attack livestock and drink their blood. Whoa, okay. They are described as dog-reptile-alien-like with a

RIP
REST IN PEACE

vicious appetite. Chupacabras are seen mostly in Central and South America, but some sightings have been reported in North America too.

CRYPTID 7:
The Wampus Cat

Seen mostly in the American South, the Wampus Cat is a large, cat-like creature with glowing red eyes. There aren't many reports in real life, but plenty of instances in popular culture, such as in *James and the Giant Peach* and *Harry Potter*. And there are multiple schools in the American South with the

Wampus Cat as their mascot! If the Wampus Cats are real, they've got a stellar PR team working for them.

CRYPTID 8:
Werewolves

Not to be confused with a regular wolf, a Werewolf is actually a man (funny . . . we haven't met many female cryptids . . .) who turns into a wolf at night. The transformations are said to only happen on nights with a full moon. There are many reported ways to become a Werewolf yourself, such as sleeping

outside under a full moon, wearing a wolfskin at night, or drinking water collected from a wolf's footprint. Best of luck to all our Werewolf-hopefuls!

CRYPTID 9:
Jackalopes

Not to burst anyone's bubble, but it seems like no one really takes the Jackalope seriously. Part jackrabbit, part antelope, these creatures can be found in folk stories and tall tales, but most often they're seen hanging on a wall, taxidermied, thanks to deer antlers being grafted onto a jackrabbit's head. There's not much more to say about these cryptids, poor unbelieved buddies.

CRYPTID 10:
Thunderbirds

The Thunderbird comes from Native American folklore. It is a powerful, revered spirit that takes the form of a bird, and thunder is said to come from its flapping wings and lightning from its beak. Thunderbirds are depicted in art and totem poles from various tribes across North America.

The most beautiful of our cryptids yet, the Thunderbird lives on.

CRYPTID 11:
Wendigos

Another cryptid from Native American mythology, but decidedly less revered, the Wendigo is a cannibalistic monster. It smells terrible, looks sickly and scary, and, if you see it, can only mean bad things are coming. Wendigos can possess people, causing them to become cannibals too. So, maybe keep your distance if ever you cross paths with one.

CRYPTID 12:
The Fresno Nightcrawler

Seen first in Fresno, California, the nightcrawler is said to be a tall, skinny human-like creature with no arms. Even newer on the scene than El Chupacabra, sightings only began in 2014. The intent and significance of the Fresno Nightcrawler is still unknown, so keep an eye on these creepy Californian Cryptids . . .

who knows where they will pop up next.

CRYPTID 13:
The Kraken

For our final cryptid, we'll swim over to the Scandinavian waters where there is said to be a giant octopus-like monster: the Kraken. Since the 1800s, there's been stories of this giant tentacled beast overtaking ships and wreaking havoc in the seas. Most people think the early sightings were probably just of a giant squid, which, to be fair, does look like a crazy sea monster.

In Cryptid Conclusion

That concludes our introduction to thirteen of our favorite cryptids. We hope you've learned a thing or two, and if nothing else, just remember: it's a big, big world. You never know what's out there. Keep your eyes open and your gullibility in check!